Withdrawals

Teresa Tarpley

Published by/distributed
Radical Women
DBA
PO Box 32
Granbury, TX
76048
www.radicalwomen.com

Radical Women

Published by Radical Women

Cover design by Lisa Bell DBA Radical Women

Printed in the USA

Print ISBN: 979-8988648529

E-book ISBN: 979-8988648536

This book is dedicated to people going through a physical and mental breakdown, not just from drugs, alcohol and cigarettes, but from unforgiveness, molestation, grief and much more.

Jesus answered and said to him, "Truly, truly, I say to you, unless one is born again he cannot see the kingdom of God."
Nicodemus said to Him, "How can a man be born when he is old? He cannot enter a second time into his mother's womb and be born, can he?"
Jesus answered, "Truly, truly, I say to you, unless one is born of water and the Spirit he cannot enter into the kingdom of God. That which is born of the flesh is flesh, and that which is born of the Spirit is spirit."

Contents

Acknowledgments

I WANT TO THANK God, the Father, the Son, and the Holy Ghost for exposing things in me I didn't realize lay buried deep within me.

Thank you to family and friends who stand beside me, even with my faults, and speak truth in love to help with recognizing those things in me God wants to remove and heal.

CHAPTER ONE

Withdrawals

I'M NOT ALONE IN having experienced pain in my life. After many years, I figured out God could heal me from pain. In desperation, I turned to Him because I couldn't stand the wounds of my past any longer. You've been there too, and many of you sought the Lord for healing. He is faithful to answer our prayers when we ask.

I thought He healed me from a lot of hurt—wounds so deep no person could touch them. And He did. In so many ways, He came in and stitched up those deep cuts, poured oil on them, and sent me on my way. We went through so much work; I thought He healed me from every possible thing there.

He didn't.

Yes, we went deep into my heart, and He kept revealing and healing. I reached a point where I didn't see anything possible I needed healed.

But God works in mysterious ways.

One day, I received a request to notarize a paper at the nursing home where my dad lived when he passed. No big deal. Drop by, witness the signature, add my name and seal, collect the fee, and done. On my way and back to life with a few extra dollars.

While there, nothing significant happened. I finished and walked out to my car. Sitting behind the steering wheel, I had a breakdown moment.

I couldn't stop crying. My heart weighed me down like lead. After wiping away tears and getting some control, my heart still ached, so I rode around his old house and the neighborhood where he hung out. Every minute I drove felt like an hour. Aware of things around me, a fog covered my brain, leaving tears flowing down my cheeks. I never lived with him in that neighborhood, but I felt his presence in every inch, because I knew he lived there.

I survived that day and made it home, exhausted for no visible reason. I washed my face, tried to encourage myself, but the weight still kept my heart from singing in joy.

Later, I reached out to a pastor, told him the situation, and asked that he pray for me.

After listening, he responded with a soft, caring voice. "Wow. I will be praying. This is the time for God to finish helping you purge out all the pain. You've gone through so much. Since then, you probably didn't have time to get it all out. But God is taking you higher now, so he is healing you."

I said, "Amen, I receive it."

After disconnecting the call, I thought about the pastor's words. Could it be I still had areas God needed to heal? Did I have areas where I still had to battle for healing and freedom? I didn't see how.

Although I never yearned for my old life of drugs or alcohol after I gave it to God, I knew people who fell repeatedly. I remembered the days when I withdrew for a while and went back for a fix, giving in to the addiction.

With addiction, you face a process, and for some they take only a baby step at a time. They have to relearn life without the addiction—whatever it looks like, and that means sometimes dealing with layers. As these thoughts drifted though my mind, light shined into my heart. This whole healing thing differed little from overcoming addictions.

Then God gave me the title for this book. *Withdrawals.*

CHAPTER TWO

Tired of Crying

"For as he thinketh in his heart, so is he:"
Proverbs 23:7a

SOMETIMES, I FOUND MYSELF laughing, cracking jokes, always asking someone to babysit my "17" kids and find out who's their daddies.

I reached a point where I regularly planned a day to pamper myself—get my hair done, treat myself to a manicure and pedicure, and then go shopping. Calling one of my homegirls, I'd see if she was available. We'd go to lunch, hangout, and have fun. I wore a cheerful face, and honestly, I enjoyed those days.

Yet during it all, I purposely neglected putting on those beautiful, long eye-lashes to complete my look. I didn't want to cry them off.

Everything looked good on the surface, but I never knew why my heart felt so heavy. For no reason, tears came out of nowhere, overflowing and running down my cheeks. I had no answer for why it happened, and I didn't want to feel weak. Worst of all, I didn't know how to explain the ache in my heart behind those tears.

After some time, I realized God lived within the hole in my soul right beside the wounds from my past.

Let me assure you, God hears tears.

When they slip unwillingly down my cheeks without a single sob, He hears them. When I wipe away a single, wayward drop, He knows. And when I sob into my pillow at night, He needs no words to understand my pain.

The more I cried, the more he heard me, and prompted me to receive His healing touch.

To draw closer to the Lord during this time, I listened to gospel music; Donald Lawrence and Le'Andria Johnson singing "Lord Deliver Me" or Kelly Price's "I Need a Healing for my Soul." While they helped and soothed me, I needed more than tears and touching music.

When I went to church, I heard, "By His stripes you are healed (Isaiah 53.5)." Each week, as the altar call came at the end of the service, my heart raced, knowing I needed to go forward and let someone pray over me for spiritual and emotional healing. But I didn't want to go. Pride fought against the urge and held me in my place. Perhaps if I'd let go of my ego and shared the sorrow with a prayer warrior, I could have gotten past it faster.

Through the years, God provided so much healing. How could I go to the front of the church and tell anyone I didn't have my life as together as what I presented—even wrote about?

Apparently, I forgot the words of Jesus. "Again I say unto you, that if two of you shall agree on earth as touching anything that they shall ask, it shall be done for them of my Father which is in heaven. For where two or three are gathered together in my name, there am I in the midst of them." (Matthew 18:19-20).

I hate to admit I cringed against the very thought of looking weak. Instead, I left services each week, my heart still heavy and not knowing how to change anything—and always leaving those eyelashes at home.

But I pressed my way through. I didn't give myself over to anything negative. I refused to let anything stop me from staying and doing only the positive.

Even though I grew tired of crying, begging God for revelation because I didn't understand so much, I kept pushing forward. When I caught a glimpse of His purpose behind one thing, another layer appeared. Again, I hit my knees, turned on the gospel music, and cried and begged again, always convincing myself to move forward.

I loved reading Joyce Meyer's book *Battlefield of the Mind* and T. D. Jakes's *Woman Thou Art Loosed*. Both touched my soul, and God used their words to minister to my soul. More than once, I pictured myself in those books.

Many people live in pain, hiding their wounds behind multiple things—good, godly things, even. If we stay busy enough, we don't have to deal with our internal thoughts and feelings.

Oh yeah, I remember a lot of hurt behind the drugs, cigarettes, alcohol, sex, etc. Those things didn't cause the pain—well, maybe they caused some of it. But they numbed the deeper pain I couldn't heal for myself. Despite the years of addictions and breaking free from them, the pain remained inside me. I might have kicked the habit of many addictions, and certainly, God healed more wounds than I could imagine. Sometimes, you gotta go deeper, and if you aren't ready or don't want to visit some of those places, God won't take you there—yet.

It doesn't matter how long ago something or someone hurt you. The pain doesn't magically disappear.

In His mercy and grace, dependent on His timing and my readiness, God waits to heal and deliver me so I can go to the next level. Most of the time, it's more about Him waiting for me.

Am I ready?

Yes, let's go.

Goodbye past.

Once more, I face tears. But this time, those tears bring healing and peace, not a repeated begging for understanding. When I surrender and ask for healing, Holy Spirit comes in and does His work.

I had to encourage myself by saying, "Teresa, there's nothing wrong with crying."

I grew up believing only the weak cried. But even Jesus wept, and I could never call him weak. Tears cleanse the soul, and all the junk inside escapes through them. Even while crying, praise God for deliverance from the hurts of your past. Then you can receive the blessings he plans for your future.

Finished with His healing (at least for now), I'm on a whole other level. My next tears will be tears of joy.

Have you ever lived with mold in your house? Doesn't matter what color of mold, once you have it, trying to rid yourself of the pest takes work—layers of work. About the time you think you got every bit of mold from your house, boom! Up pops another spot—usually when and where you least expect it.

You scrub some more, thinking, "Finally, I got it all."

Later you pull back the shower curtain or open that closet door, and a big ugly spot peeps out at you almost smiling (if mold could smile), and laughs because you never saw it growing there.

Gross example, but bear with me. God gave me this example of mold to explain what I endured during these times of additional healing.

After reading and surrendering to instruction from the Bible, the healing didn't always feel real. As I forgave and sought forgiveness for clinging to hurt, new revelations kept popping up. Just like that nasty mold none of us want in our homes. I realized I still had a lot of mold God wanted to purge out of me.

Once I'm totally healed and delivered, then God can make me holy and whole. Shoot. And I thought that happened way back when I wrote my first book, *Heartbroken: Now Healed and Delivered.*

Could it be that until I leave Earth, I'll go through more of this process? Probably. Besides, in their brokenness, people still hurt others, so I suspect I need to deal with new wounds as soon as they happen. Praise God I know that, so at least the mold doesn't get out of hand and overwhelm me before God ends it.

Let it go so you can grow. Stop focusing on the pain and focus on the promise of God to keep your mind positive when you want to think or speak negatively. At that moment, tell the negative to exit.

CHAPTER THREE

Still Here

DURING THE PAST YEARS, I got over a lot of stuff like unforgiveness, toxic love, and wondering. At least I thought I did.

I kept wondering, "Why I can't get to the next level?"

Maybe you know how I felt. Maybe you wonder the same thing. Years of working through hurt, letting God come in and heal those places. I should be at a higher level. And in many ways, I am. But something holds me back. I don't understand.

As I moved forward, God opened doors, but I sensed He had more for me, and people spoke that over me. So what kept me from experiencing that higher level? I dealt with all that stuff, right?

Unfortunately, I had a bunch of crap still here—buried in my heart so deep I didn't see it. If you ever watched the *Hoarders* television show, you know they don't clean everything out in one day. They find so much trash, junk, unmentionable horrors in those layers. So, they attack one later at a time. They clean out layer after layer after layer. And sometimes, the person who hoards it all doesn't want them to take out a stack of papers hiding a dead rat.

Okay. Grossness over, but you get the picture. Our hearts can be that way—full of unforgiveness. We clean up that one or ten incidents and think we're good. But then, God moves a layer of pain, and the unforgiveness oozes up to the surface. Yuck. We gotta clean up that layer. It's like piles of trash inside our hearts, and until we surrender to God, that trash grows and rots.

You gotta take that trash to the dumpster and let God clean you so you can receive the blessing God has for you. You gotta let go so you can grow.

While I let go of things and found grace to forgive others, I didn't realize I still held tight to unforgiveness toward myself—mostly from my past and how I treated my kids. The most difficult person for me to forgive might be myself.

Those memories of myself tore at my heart. I prayed, asking God to teach me how to forgive myself. I didn't know how. Even after my children forgave me, I couldn't. Then again, the devil likes it when we cover ourselves in shame.

Just like Jesus told the adulterous women in the Bible, "I forgive you, now forgive yourself."

That's what he told me. If God can forgive me, who am I not to forgive myself? It took me a long time to move that belief from my head to my heart.

Oh, yes, it was a more than a challenge.

I often encourage others to forgive themselves, but applying what you know to your situation doesn't always come as easy as you make it sound. With those same words I used to encourage other, I encouraged myself. And sometime, I spoke the words out loud.

"Teresa, you made mistakes. You learned from them. You weren't as mature as you are now. At least you can own up to your faults. If others don't forgive you, that's on them. Stop allowing your past to drag you down."

Unforgiveness can drag you into depression if you let it—and that applies to whether you need to forgive others or yourself.

Spirits of shame, condemnation, and depression hit me day and night. While I don't go looking for demons behind every door, I believe they exist, and they love to play with a person's mind—especially one who wants to walk closely with the Lord. So, I told those spirits to exit out of my life.

The Bible says if you resist the devil, he will flee (James 4:7). In other words, when he comes knocking on the door of your mind and emotions, tell him to get lost. And he will. As Christians, we don't always remember that we can overcome this terrible enemy of ours. He has no right to defeat us, but if we let him come in and park himself on the sofa, he will. When we say, "So long, sucker!" he must leave.

The Apostle Paul wrote to Christians at Philippi, encouraging them to forget those things behind them and press toward the mark of the higher calling in Christ (Philippians 3:13-14). If you forgot, or never knew, Paul lived a godly life, instructing others in how to walk like

Jesus. But it wasn't always so. In the beginnings of what people then called "The Way," Paul persecuted and killed Christians. Recorded in the book of Acts (7:58-8:1), Paul stood by and held coats for the "religious" leaders who stoned Stephen, the first to die for his belief in Jesus.

Paul became a pursuer of the first Christians, seeking to lock them up and, yes, kill them. Imagine how he felt even after an up-close-and-personal encounter with Jesus? He knew God forgave him, but I wonder if those memories and the inability to forgive himself might have been the thorn in the flesh he talked about in 2 Corinthians 12.

To win the race of life, we have to quit looking behind and press forward to the finish line. Ever watch someone running—in reality or in a movie? When the person looks back, it never fails—face plant on the pavement. That's true of our emotions and spirits. We can't look behind and not expect to lose the race and get beaten up along the way.

My mom was single for a long time, and I remember her saying she was tired of being lonely. Trust me—I understand how she felt. I been there. Some of you reading, go ahead and nod. You feel it too.

I had to learn to love myself. You can't do that when you refuse to forgive yourself for the past and rid yourself of any junk still hanging around your heart.

Tell that spirt of loneliness to get out. It's over!

Learn how to speak positive words and thoughts over yourself and tell all the negative junk to exit, because you own a whole new positive level and no negative can go with you.

Goodbye past. Hello future.

CHAPTER FOUR

Isolation

THE FIRST PRESIDENT OF Indonesia, Sukarno, said, "The worst cruelty that can be inflicted on a human being is isolation."

We can all identify with isolation, especially after dealing with it during the pandemic on a larger scale than at any time in history. In the past, such as when polio ran rampant or during plagues or widespread viruses, people with the diseases went into isolation to protect those around them.

Some cultures use isolation for prisoners of war to demoralize and keep them from communicating. Interestingly, prisoners often find ways around the isolation to "talk" with each other. Even in modern-day prisons, inmates sometimes end up in isolation for their protection or because they still want to hurt others.

While long-term isolation can destroy a person, even lead to death, not all isolation hurts us. Sometimes, God will put you in a quiet place—only you and Him. In that period of isolation, He can deal with our hearts and minds.

Isolation may last for a few minutes, a day, a week, or however long we need to accomplish what God wants to do in us. Various artists spend much time in isolation to complete their work, but even the most introverted person eventually wants to come out and play amongst the living.

I never liked the idea of isolation until I realized God wanted to use it for my breakthrough in this fight of withdrawals.

Sometimes, I arrived at work before time to clock in. Surrounded by people, I sat in silence with my headphones on, listening to gospel music. Not my usual style. Co-workers expected me to clown around, laughing, and talking about babysitting my 17 kids.

Many asked what was wrong? Some wanted to jump all over the one who upset me. Of course, no one did anything to me.

God showed me He had to put me in a place of isolation so I could be healed and delivered.

That caught me off guard, because I thought He'd already delivered me. But in peeling back fresh layers of painful places, He needed to isolate me. Sometimes, you still have unforgiveness and hatred based on your past. Like a serious illness, that infection of the soul can spread to others in your circles. God must isolate you so you won't pass your infection to someone else who has nothing to do with what you're going through.

Ever been around a person who oozes misery? Someone so full of hurt that it squirts from them and lands all over you? In our moments of pain, we always hurt the ones nearest us. We may not realize how we damage someone we care about because all we see is our pain.

In situations of physical withdrawal from drugs or alcohol, a person lashes out at anyone who comes near. He or she may scratch, hit, kick, or puke all over another person. Unintentional, but painful all the same.

Like a contagious disease, we can't help spreading the junk inside of us from past wounds. We may be unaware of a painful situation buried inside, but everyone around us eventually sees it come out, and usually it happens when we spew all over them.

In His grace, God isolates us so we don't destroy others with our infected heart, hurting our relationships beyond repair at times. That's what He did for me.

I deleted and blocked people on social media. I erased numbers stored in my phone or ignored calls, because I needed healing. In some cases, those people created toxicity in my life, and I can never add them back. But that doesn't mean I kept myself isolated permanently.

While hurting, I simply couldn't have all my friends in my life, for their sake and mine.

Never trust your tongue when your heart aches. Hush till you heal. And if necessary, put yourself in isolation for a time.

CHAPTER FIVE

Detox

"No one puts new wine into old wineskins; otherwise, the wine will burst the skins, and the wine is lost and the skins as well; but one puts new wine into fresh wineskins."

Mark 2:22

I DON'T KNOW MUCH about wine making, and who uses wineskins any longer? I'm not sure if glass bottles work the same way, but when Jesus used the example recorded in Mark, the people knew exactly what he meant.

They didn't have glass bottles back then, so after making wine, they put it in leather "bottles" to ferment. During the process, the wineskins expanded, growing with the wine. After use, they had no more capacity to expand. While people could store other liquids in those containers, putting in new wine resulted in a wineskin trying to expand, but instead bursting.

His message, intended for the Pharisees (religious leaders bent on following harsh rules), meant they needed a fresh perspective and understanding of what God intended to do.

Enough of the lesson on Mark 2:22, except to say, to detox, we need to shift our mindset to a better way of living.

Detox (short for detoxification) requires a process or a period during which a person abstains from or rids the body of toxic or unhealthy substances. Our minds picture a person going through withdrawal from drugs or alcohol.

But if you think about it, going through detox doesn't always include drugs, alcohol, and cigarettes. While our brain immediately goes to the physical, God thinks in spiritual terms. He may very well take you through detox from physically harmful substances, but He looks beyond the body and goes straight to the heart.

My past is no secret, so anyone who knows me can attest to the physical detox I faced. Many of you have or will experience the agony of coming down off drugs, alcohol, and cigarettes when you follow Jesus. Not a simple task—one almost impossible to achieve without God's grace. So, I understand physical detoxing.

It took me a long time to see my need for a spiritual detoxification.

I must admit, God is detoxing me from multiple things as I write this. Again, I thought he already delivered me from them. But as with physical additions, it can take a long time to complete the detox and finally walk away from my addictions.

Of course, it's painful. This junk has been in me for so long. But you gotta let go to get to the next level. No matter how difficult or how much it hurts, you press in just like an alcoholic who declares no more and fights through the physical agony.

Any detox leaves you tired, sad, depressed, and without an appetite. True of physical detox, but also of a spiritual one.

I hung on to things that were hard to let go of. As I fought the pain, I wanted to cling to those emotions until the Holy Spirit pried them from my clenched hands.

Once God gave me perspective, I wanted to accept it, but I had to learn the new way—the fresh wineskins.

I had an older car—not the greatest, but it ran well, and I could afford the payments. After a no-fault-of-mine accident, the insurance paid it off. Someone blessed me with funds for a down payment on a new car. Overjoyed, I chose a newer model, thankful for God's provision.

Even though I knew how to drive, I had to learn that new car. The old car needed a key to crank—the new car didn't. I won't bore you with all the other details, but it took time, and as strange as it seems, I had moments where I missed that old car. But you better believe I more than wanted to let it go, so I could have something better.

You gotta be willing to walk out of your past and step into your new. Ain't no future in the back. During my detox, all those thoughts came out in writing, and of course, I shared them.

Before God finished with my detox process, I learned to improve the way I encourage others and how to encourage myself.

Encouragers need to encouragement. You never know when they may be ridding themselves of toxic waste, too.

CHAPTER SIX

Jealousy

I OFTEN WONDERED WHY I always supported people, calling to check in on them. Nobody seemed to check on me—until they need something. Early in life, I taught myself this bad habit of standing by men especially. If I had nothing, they disappeared. Eventually, I figured this out about men who use women, and it didn't seem difficult to break that habit.

Unfortunately, it didn't stop me from giving to others who needed my support without giving back. It took a long time to see the unequal relationships in my life. I walked around like a failed bank—giving out emotionally, spiritually, and yes, sometimes with my physical possessions, but never receiving a deposit in return.

Afterward, they hung out with everybody but me. No wonder I got so down. Emotional bankruptcy drains you. Lost and alone, I trudged through life, trying to stay positive and keep giving to others. How do you give when your tank's running on empty?

That pain grew, consuming so much of me. I hid it from others, but at home or in my car, the tears poured from my soul. When I was down, I had no one to turn to. Sometimes, I even felt like God didn't love me. If He did, why did I go through so much pain?

Do you ever ask that question? Or maybe you ask a different question. I asked these, too. Why does everybody doing wrong have good stuff happen to them? But the people trying to do right? I ain't seeing nothing good happening to them.

Deep inside, I know that isn't always true, but it sure feels that way—especially when you're in the middle of despair, trying to climb up to a higher level and getting nowhere. I prayed with more sincerity than ever before. It seemed the harder I prayed for anything, everyone around me saw answers to their prayers. But nothing changed for me, and I often doubted God heard any of my prayers. If He heard, why didn't I see answers?

It took time, but I finally understood His timing isn't mine, and as a loving Father, He doesn't always say yes to my prayers. Either way, I must trust Him, and when He makes a promise, it may take a long time, but He will keep that promise.

I read Psalms 37, tears flooding my eyes every time. It hit my spirit with the force of a sledgehammer. The words sank deep in my heart as I identified with King David.

In the grip of the Word, I cried out to God, not knowing what to say. But God heard my tears. The Psalm comforted me in knowing I'm not the only one who ever felt this way. Sometimes, we don't get an immediate answer, but I knew He understood and held me close while I wept.

Not long after that, I talked to a lady, telling her I felt like I didn't have anybody. Lonely, depressed, I even had thoughts of suicide. Of course, I left that piece of information out.

Later that day, while driving, God reminded me of a person who asked what I want for my birthday or Mother's Day?

I said, "I'm not worried about nothing. Long as I can hear your voice, it's a blessing."

Eye opening moment. I didn't care enough about myself to admit if I wanted anything. Yes, someone's love meant more to me than any gift, but that's not the point. I expected nothing in return.

While giving without receiving isn't necessarily bad, some people take advantage of it, and they can only do it when we allow it.

Simple truth—I encouraged others to use me.

At the same time, God revealed I had a lot of jealousy about what others had that I didn't. When I saw friends out laughing and enjoying each other's company, I longed for sweet fellowship. If I saw a couple on a date, it made me sad I didn't have it. Even a nice car and house could make me cringe with envy.

There's a reason God included not wanting what others have in His original Ten Commandments. "You shall not covet your neighbor's house; you shall not covet your neighbor's wife or his male servant or his female servant or his ox or his donkey or anything that belongs to your neighbor." (Exodus 20:17)

When we want what someone else has, after a time, that desire consumes us, and it opens a door to the spirit of jealousy. If that spirit takes root, we can't help but grow depressed and lonely.

Instead of turning to God for all I needed, I looked at others. I opened the door for many to use me, so they would love me. But using someone doesn't mean you love him or her. And you will always find people who have more or less than you do.

I thank God for exposure to these truths in my life. I needed that.

In response to His revelations that day, I prayed and asked God to purge jealousy out of me.

Some of this tied back to my addiction to pleasing people, which I talk more about in the next chapter. To make everyone else happy, I gave away too much and drained myself. Empty, I had to confess I still carried some of that addiction. I needed to let God break it off me. Through the pain, I saw hope, but not without change.

Going through withdrawals is excruciating. In the midst of it all, healing and wisdom break through the pain. You gotta let go and allow God to take over so you can heal and grow.

On the other side of the withdrawal from pleasing people in an unhealthy way, God poured out blessings on me. No, I don't have all those things—yet. But instead of looking at what I don't have, I thank Him for all He has given me.

CHAPTER SEVEN

Still a People Pleaser

EVERY DAY, I READ the following verses.

Galatians 1:10—"For am I now seeking the favor of men, or of God? Or am I striving to please men? If I were still trying to please men, I would not be a bond-servant of Christ."

1 Corinthians 9-19—"For though I am free from all men, I have made myself a slave to all, so that I may win more."

Acts 5:29—"But Peter and the apostles answered, 'We must obey God rather than men.'"

Matthew 12:47-50—"Someone said to Him, 'Behold, Your mother and Your brothers are standing outside seeking to speak to You.' But Jesus answered the one who was telling Him and said, 'Who is My mother and who are My brothers?' And stretching out His hand toward His disciples, He said, 'Behold My mother and My brothers!

For whoever does the will of My Father who is in heaven, he is My brother and sister and mother.'"

After writing my book, *Why Y'all Treat Me So Bad* (Radical Women, 2021), I thought I overcame being a people pleaser. Not so. Like all addictions, this one came with layers, too.

I still had an issue of encouraging folks to use me when they needed something. When they were down, I heard from them all the time, but when they got up on their feet, they were gone. Not like my younger years when this scenario always involved a man I wanted to keep around, but equally devastating.

I had to learn—not their fault. What? People using me, not their fault. But they used me. Yes, they did.

But—I allowed it to happen.

Check this out. Certain people called me, asking for help to get out of a sticky situation. When I told them I wasn't available to help, they stopped talking to me. Not just for a while, but done with me forever.

My heart ached to reject them, but at that moment, I couldn't offer any help. Either I didn't have the time or money—I seriously could do nothing. Had they called a week later, I might have helped. But God times things perfectly. And the requests came when He knew I had to say no.

After that, I wondered what I did wrong? Why didn't they talk to me anymore? Flashbacks of my younger years with all the dudes using me until I had no money haunted me. Then I understood. In the same way I let those men use me, I allowed anyone needing help to use me, too.

Interestingly, I believed God wanted me to help others—that He included that in my ministry calling. Yes, He called me to do that, but not for them to use me until I had nothing left. See, the devil likes to take truth and twist and use it against us. He makes them half-truths to serve his purpose and draw us away from God instead of to Him.

Realizing the full truth, I had to encourage myself the way I encourage others. As usual, I spoke the words of encouragement out loud.

"Teresa, stop giving your all to people. Focus on God first, take care of yourself, and stop worrying about people."

Withdrawal from any addiction doesn't come without pain and commitment to stick with it. As I withdrew from always pleasing people, the backlash came with it. I can't stop what people feel and say about me.

The ones using me don't like this change, and they don't always say nice things. Going through withdrawal from people is hard. Some things are traditional for people, even myself. I've known many people all my life, and I want to stay connected to them, if possible, but I also need good boundaries for them and myself.

It could even be family members who use you and have for years. That makes it more difficult and painful. You gotta let them go. Everybody can't go to your next level. Every relationship is not a lifetime contract. I'm not supposed to take care of everyone for my entire life.

For their sake, let go and stop babying people. If they don't fall, they never know what getting up is like. Besides, you gotta let them go, so they can grow.

Imagine having a baby and never letting them scoot around, crawl or learn to walk. They fall—lots. But without trying, they never walk. Would you want your child to never learn to walk? Of course, not. Support them, pick them up and brush them off, encourage them to try again. But quit doing everything for them. You can't, and it isn't best for them, either.

I learned to stop pleasing people.

I'm on a whole other level. Being addicted to people and knowing what to do for them is worse than being addicted to drugs. It hurts to let go, but you gotta go through withdrawals to heal and move forward again.

Pleasing people? No more. So long—bye-bye.

If God tells me to help someone for a moment, okay. But I do it to please Him, not that person. And if He says no or stop, then I obey even if it hurts to do so. He wants what's best for me, and what's best for that person.

Think about the worst time in life God brought you out of. If he brought you out of that horrible thing and time, this ain't nothing.

Start telling the negative to exit and start moving forward. Not always easy. That addiction calls out, tries to woo me back. I reach for it, and say, "NO!"

Making a choice, I purposely quit going back to what God disconnected me from. And sometimes that means breaking free from a person who might need to stand on his or her own for a change.

"A wise man will hear and increase in learning, and a man of understanding will acquire wise counsel." (Proverbs 1:5)

"Peace I leave with you; My peace I give to you; not as the world gives do I give to you. Do not let your heart be troubled, nor let it be fearful." (John 14:27)

CHAPTER EIGHT

Still a Gossiper

"Therefore, if anyone is in Christ, he is a new creature; the old things passed away; behold, new things have come."

2 Corinthians 5:17

PEOPLE DO YOU WRONG. It happens.

As much as I want to go straight to that forgiveness thing, sometimes, I found myself with issues over what someone did to me.

Not proud of it, but I would squat down in my feelings, finding myself complaining to others about what that person did to me. I didn't do a good job of going to the person and confronting what he or she did or how it left me feeling. I could rant on for days to multiple people about how awful that person treated me.

Until a harsh reality hit me like a rock. I wasn't affecting them and making them look bad. I made myself look bad.

But doesn't it matter that someone hurt me? That someone mistreated me or took advantage of me?

Of course, it matters. But telling everyone what they did does no good. It only makes people want to avoid you so they don't hear the same story all over again. It makes you come across as a negative, bitter person.

You know that person, right? The one that makes you cringe when his or her name pops up on the caller ID? Yeah, that one. You know if you answer, for the next hour you'll hear the same junk you been hearing for months—maybe years. Nothing changed. That person didn't confront the one who wronged him or her. And that oozing wound just gets more stinky.

I don't want to talk to THAT person.

Oops. What if I am THAT woman? By the grace of God, no. Yet I could see myself turning into that gossiper.

I grew up with gossip—all the time. And I never wanted to become such a woman. We fall into that trap far too easily, don't we?

You know, gossip doesn't stop when you open that door. After your call, that friend calls up someone else, and the conversation goes from what happened to you to how you won't let it go. And it grows from there. Before long, someone leaves off what happened to you, and the gossip becomes how you are so negative all the time. That's the nature of gossip.

As I pondered this thought about not gossiping, God took me back to a time at one of my jobs. Some co-workers often came around, wanting to gossip and complain about another co-worker. Not wanting to take part in gossip, I tuned them out with gospel music.

Well, guess what? I'm back at it—tuning out those words about others. And God forgive me if I instigate the gossip.

Keep in mind, the Bible says, "The effective prayers of a righteous man can accomplish much" (James 5:16b). Jesus said, "Do not judge so that you will not be judged." (Matthew 7:1)

When you gossip, you judge. Far better to pray for the one who hurt you than to judge him or her.

God showed me, instead of gossiping and complaining, pray for those who hurt you. I also had to pray, asking God to teach me how not to gossip and complain. I didn't know how to break such a strong human tendency.

Of course, He answered that prayer. I suspect He loves it when we ask for help to learn His ways directly from the One who perfected those ways. I don't always get it right, but He gives me opportunities to practice.

I also put the positive over the negative. If a person wronged me, I asked them to forgive me. Yeah, I know—backwards in some of your minds. Still, I took offense. Asking for their forgiveness frees me, and it may restore our relationship instead of breaking it.

Many times, I misunderstood what they said or did. Even if I didn't, I can forgive because God forgave me. And He might use my humble spirit to change them.

Then, regardless of the outcome, I write his or her name, lay it beside Psalms 37, and focus on myself and what God needs to change in me.

CHAPTER NINE

Unforgiveness

"When you stand praying, forgive if you have anything against anyone, so that your Father who is in heaven will also forgive you your transgressions. But if you do not forgive, neither will your Father who is in heaven forgive your transgressions.

Mark 11:25-26

LET ME TELL YOU, having unforgiveness in your heart leads to addictions of bitterness and even rage. Once those roots take hold, you keep going back for more, letting the unforgiveness feed the addiction.

Talk about something that seems impossible. Forgiving someone for what he or she did to you is hard. The worse the offense, the harder to forgive.

I didn't realize I had hatred in my heart. As I wrote books about my life, I kept dealing with memories as they came up. But I didn't understand that I still had to battle hatred toward someone I knew for a long time.

Years ago, someone played me. We talked, and I thought we worked through it all. I never thought about that incident any more—until he reached out to me.

Memories overtook me, along with a flood of emotions. I cried out to God. Why did He let anyone do me like that?

I couldn't stop thinking about this person, wanting to bash the one who hurt me so badly.

Then, God showed me some more memories—ones I liked even less than those recalling how badly someone wounded me. In these other memories, I saw myself, at times, doing people the way that one did me.

Truthfully, I still had some good bassing in mind, but I had to encourage myself that two wrongs don't make a right. Besides, I would affect myself more than anyone else.

A beautiful line from *Diary of a Mad Black Woman*, spoken by Cicely Tyson as Myrtle tugs at my mind. "You've got to forgive him; not for him, but for you." The beautiful Ms. Tyson explains how those who hurt you take power over you, but by refusing to forgive, you let them keep that power. One of the most powerful lines from Myrtle ends the scene. "Forgive him baby, and after you forgive him, forgive yourself." (Thank you, Tyler Perry.) [1]

God exposed another hidden addiction in me. Unforgiveness. I didn't have to deal with this person for so many years, and I didn't know so much bitterness hid below the surface. Just talking on the phone triggered the memory, and I had to get on my knees, forgive the person, then seek God's forgiveness and forgive myself for clinging to it for so long.

God allows situations to happen so he can expose myself to me. I had to surrender to him and heal from that deep, long-ago wound.

I can't imagine getting down on my knees, asking God to forgive me for my sins only to hear Him say, "Heck no. I can't cause, Teresa, you won't forgive others for what they did to you."

Even though God helped me forgive many people before, this one hurt more. In unfamiliar territory, I again cried out and asked God to teach me how to forgive. I forgave some people, but never something so deep and buried for so long—something I forgot about because I ignored it.

Even though my heart remained heavy, I continued praying while going through withdrawals from unforgiveness and the accompanying bitterness and rage.

I thought forgiving others was hard. But as I said many times before, forgiving myself was even harder. Every time I had to forgive someone else, I remembered the things I

1. (Cicely Tyson 2005)

did in my past. As I prayed, asking God to teach me how to forgive myself, God reminded of a biblical concept.

"I forgive you; now forgive yourself."

Editor's Note: Although no Bible verse says specifically "forgive yourself," John 8:11 points to Jesus telling the woman caught in adultery, "Neither do I condemn you. Go and sin no more." In 1 John 9:11, the Bible clearly promises that when we seek forgiveness, God is faithful to forgive us. If God can forgive us, we can forgive ourselves. Like that woman in the New Testament times who faced death, we go and sin no more, accepting God's forgiveness and walking in His ways after that.

CHAPTER TEN

Big Mouth Shut Up; You Talk Too Much

"He who restrains his words has knowledge, and he who has a cool spirit is a man of understanding. Even a fool, when he keeps silent, is considered wise; when he closes his lips, he is considered prudent."
Proverbs 17:27-28

AFTER REALIZING AND ADMITTING I was a gossiper and complainer, God revealed the next surprise addiction I needed to break.

I talk too much.

That's harsh. I didn't want to hear something like that, but I listened as God exposed not only the addiction, but the explanation behind it.

Every time I went places such as the store or called somebody on the phone, I always opened the conversation with, "I got some good news for you."

People love hearing good news, right? How's that such a terrible thing? For over 15-20 minutes, I talked, sharing the good news, but not necessarily without other things before or after. They are trying to go, and I keep steadily talking. When they finally catch me stopping for a breath, they have to go.

The problem—I wanna be heard, but I don't wanna listen.

Even talking on the phone, a person might try to talk, but I cut them off.

They often said, "Go ahead and talk." Or they might've said, "I'm with my family."

Even then, I didn't respect their time. I kept talking, never stopping for a breath or to let them respond.

Eventually, they promised to call later just to get me off the phone.

I realized some people preferred I send a text, because I called too often and stayed on the phone for way too long.

One day, while talking with a friend, he said, "That's why people don't enjoy talking to you, Teresa. Because you talk too much."

I got off the phone, angry and hurt. My feelings puffed up, indignant that anyone would say such a hurtful thing. But after calming down and considering his words, I realized it was true.

I did have a big mouth!

Made me wonder if the R&B rapper Whodini was talking about me in the song "Big Mouth" or Run DMC's "You Talk Too Much." Even then, I laughed at the thought. How did those guys know me, anyway?

In the laughter, I had to check and encourage myself. I'm not meant to tell everything. Everybody ain't on my level, and they don't all get excited about my good news. What feels wonderful to me means nothing to them. I needed to move in, silent.

Another easy way I verified I talk too much was by a person's facial expression. On the phone, I could also tell by their tone of voice. Again, they would act very kind, but they would do whatever to end the call, even if they had to lie to cut the conversation off. While I talked too much, the person became distracted, barely responding. I might hear background noises as they continued with chores or work.

My incessant talking happened more often when I got upset over something. I memorized and applied Proverbs 29:11. "A fool always loses his temper; but a wise man holds it back." Retelling the offense kept my temper in an uproar.

Staying quiet and not sharing all my business with everybody took a while to learn. Just stop talking when I am upset, because, man, I can talk so much. I didn't understand what I was saying myself half the time.

You just got to be quiet and don't say nothing. Ouch. I heard the pastor say one day, "What's the use of going into your prayer closet and praying, then coming out with the same junk on your back? Leave that junk in the prayer closet. Quit taking it with you, because everywhere you go that stuff can go. If you're going to pray about it, why you going to continue to worry about it and talk about it?"

If I continue sharing it with someone else after I prayed about that situation, it means I ain't trusting in God. I'm just sitting up the continued holding on to all that baggage.

How do I say I trust and believe in God if I'm sitting there sharing my business with everyone else? That also means I'm still addicted to people.

It hit me hardest when I judged others for doing the same thing to me. I had those calls during busy moments, and I kept trying to end the call, needing to do something else. But I couldn't, because they never stopped talking. After the call ended, I fussed over the inconsideration, suddenly realizing that's how people felt about me.

I had to check myself. I ain't better than that person, so why did I judge him or her? Instead, correct myself.

At times, I talked more than Charlie Brown's teacher. "Wonk, wonk, wonk, wonk, wonk." I'm sure the person listening heard those words over what I actually said.

In dealing with this issue, I asked myself why. Why do I feel the need to keep talking? Perhaps I should dig deeper for the answer. God will expose the truth when I'm ready to hear it. For now, realizing I do it can help overcome the tendency until I get to the root of this addiction and break it for the last time.

I can't hear God when I spend all my time doing the talking.

The beauty of having God involved in my withdrawals is His patience. He doesn't take me where I'm not ready to go. But He won't leave me where I am, either. More pain may come later as He peels back yet another layer, but it won't be without His comforting presence.

CHAPTER ELEVEN

Relapse

"*Brethren, I do not regard myself as having laid hold of it yet; but one thing I do; forgetting what lies behind and reaching forward to what lies ahead, I press forward toward the goal for the prize of the upward call of God in Christ Jesus.*"

Philippians 3:13-14

RELAPSE—RETURN TO A PREVIOUS bad condition or a worse way of life after making an improvement.

I think back to when I was on crack. Admitted into a drug treatment center, I kicked the habit and didn't have any relapses while there. I left clean.

After they discharged me, I went back to buy some dope. I said, "Imma just buy me a dime rock."

Next thing, all the money's gone. Same thing happened the first time I stopped smoking cigarettes for a few months. Then, when I picked it back up, the addiction got worse.

I truly thank God for delivering me from those deadly habits. Without him, I might be dead instead of whole and living a clean, successful life.

But writing this book made me realize I didn't just relapse from crack and cigarettes.

How about gossip, complaining, negative thoughts, jealousy, and unforgiveness? Not to mention the excessive talking issue. Anytime I go back to the past God delivered me from, I don't get better. I get worse. Breaking the addiction yet again requires more work, more pain, more energy, and more everything. It always requires a greater degree of self-forgiveness, because now I know better.

Always remember, ain't no future in the back.

I can't imagine going back on crack or putting a cigarette in my mouth again. The thought disgusts me. Besides, I couldn't bear the pain my children, family and friends would endure if I relapsed into either of those things again.

Then why do I find it so easy to fall back into some of these other addictions? I'm human, and thankfully, God isn't finished with me yet.

While withdrawal from physical addictions cause genuine pain, nausea, shakes and so much more people can see, emotional and spiritual addictions hide from plain sight. We can push down the withdrawal symptoms around others, releasing them only when alone. But they often spill over without our knowledge and still affect those surrounding us.

Withdrawal from these unseen addictions hurts as bad, and unfortunately, they sometimes contain layers we can only deal with one-by-one. Unlike physical withdrawal, we may discover fresh layers that lead back to the addictions discussed in this book. That's why we press forward, like Paul wrote about to the Christians at Philippi.

God put a higher calling on my life—the Joseph anointing people spoke over me. That means, in this world, I must continue dealing with these different addictions, doing my best not to pick them back up by choice.

Life happens, and fresh woundings rip open the scarred tissue, releasing a memory of something from days, weeks, months, years, even decades ago. And against my will, I may fall back into that old addiction.

But God, in His faithfulness, reveals the root my new hurt triggered so I can deal with it. Like Paul, I press forward because I want to reach that higher level God planned for me.

Someday, I won't relapse into the same old thing again. I look forward to that day, and I'll move to a higher level with God, rejoicing.

CHAPTER TWELVE

Stuck

WHEN WE GET STUCK in the same spot for a long time, we grow very comfortable. We like the known—even if our known spot puts us in grave danger or kills our soul. Most of us don't like change, so we stay in that cozy spot, even if we need to move forward in life.

When you gotta come out of your comfort zone, things get sticky. We may only experience mild discomfort, but if leaving our favorite spot requires a more drastic change, then we may face outright torture. At least it feels like torture—the pain intensifies the more uncomfortable we get in our new zone.

Suddenly, being stuck doesn't seem all that bad. If I'm not hurting myself or anyone else, I can stay in my comfort zone and avoid all these withdrawals. Then again—staying stuck means I never get to a higher level with God or in life.

Can you imagine how a tree feels being stuck in the same spot for its lifetime? Without warning, someone decides it can't be there any longer. That tree wants to stay put—it's all the tree knows, and it stands tall and proud doing... nothing. But someone needs to move it, making room for something new, and perhaps to strip it bare, using the wood to create a beautiful, useful boat, house, furniture, or whatever.

That tree doesn't understand why it can't stay in the comfort zone where it lived since its days as a sapling. Someone gotta dig that tree out of the ground. And depending on the type of tree, the roots may cling to dirt a mile below the surface. That tree ain't letting go without a fight. Each chop sends shudders up the roots, through the trunk, and all the way to the highest branches. The tree weeps in silent pain until it finally lets go and opens up to possibilities in its new place.

Well, that's what happens in life. We gotta be dug from our comfort zone. You gotta let go so you can regrow into something more wonderful than you ever imagined.

Your digging up takes you through a healing process—and yes, it can be a long, laborious process. Once you're willing to come out of your comfort zone, you need deliverance, so you can go to a higher level.

Like Jesus told the disciples in Matthew 17, this kind can only come through fasting and prayer. God may lead you to fast and get into your prayer closet with nobody but you and Him.

In the same way you want intimacy with men, that's the same way God wants intimacy with you. We're not talking sexual here—were talking true intimacy. He'll allow things to happen that expose what's been in you for a long time. Deliverance has to take place despite your title.

Everyone's deliverance from addictions looks different. You can't experience the same thing I did, and you won't have the same roots to cut away and destroy.

Our addictions can be a long-term relationship, gossiping, etc. When God told me it was time to let go, I had to release people with long-term connections between us. The process hurt, and I didn't want to break those roots. But once I let them go, I grew. I don't care how comfortable you are in a relationship, if God tells you let it go, He knows that bond will bring you nothing but heartbreak.

You may need to let go of a job. Many people are stuck in a traditional saying—every man, every woman, every job, and every church are the same. How do you know if you haven't been with every man, woman, every job, and every church?

We make that assumption, because if we take that approach, we get to stay in our cozy little recliner, lazing our way through life. If I admit something better might exist for me, then I have to do something about it.

In the past, I had to learn how to buy new bras and panties. I got stuck in a mindset of poverty, tying my bra strings up to make them fit. I cut old stockings to make panties. Why did I do that? Because it felt comfortable, although I had so many other options that cost little.

At one time, I used salt and a towel to brush my teeth. Seriously? I could go to the Dollar Tree and buy a toothbrush and paste. I washed clothes and bathed with dishwashing liquid, if I bathed and washed the clothes. It was a learning process to change my mindset. I left that comfort zone and discovered I didn't have to skimp on simple things in life. I got stuck doing these things in my comfort zone, but when I changed, it took me to a better way of living.

I used to be stuck, but not anymore. I'm on a whole other level.

It's time to come out of your comfort zone. Let go of those comfortable but less-than-best things, so you can heal and grow.

If you've been stuck long enough, you're ready to change and step into something uncomfortable. The process will hurt, it won't come easy, and you may get tempted to go running back to the comfy little spot.

Press forward. You will never regret making the changes God asks you to make. Let go and let God so you can get beyond the sticky place and climb where God wants you to experience an upgraded comfort zone.

CHAPTER THIRTEEN

It's Over—Exit

"Therefore, if anyone is in Christ, he is a new creature; the old things passed away; behold new things have come."

2 Corinthians 5:17

EXIT—A WAY OUT, AN act of going out, leaving a place.

After all the healing God performed in me, the self-forgiveness lingered. I dealt with much of it over the years, digging out stubborn roots. I didn't realize layers of unforgiveness toward myself from my past and how I treated my children and others clung to me with a ferociousness God had to chop through repeatedly.

As He continued working, the pain seared me, breaking my heart. About the time God and my kids forgave me for one thing, I'd remember something else and go through the process again—and again—and one more time. Despite knowing God and others forgave me, I struggled with this thing of forgiving myself.

As in every other situation, I prayed for God to show me the way to forgive myself. And he did. As I stated in a previous chapter, He reminded me of the woman caught in adultery. That message to me didn't change.

But I needed to get it from my head to my heart. I still didn't know how to do that—believe in my head, know the right words and the correct churchy answers—but not apply it to myself. While I could speak this truth to others all day long, I couldn't seem to grasp it for my life—to apply personally the forgiveness I so willingly extended to others.

God reminded me, "Stop allowing your past to drag you down."

I can be stubborn sometimes.

Just as unforgiveness of others can drag you into depression, so can holding the past against yourself. I continued praying James 4:7 and Philippians 3:13-14. Forgetting what lies behind includes letting go of what I did in the past.

If God can forgive me, who am I to refuse forgiving myself?

When a song, place, or thought raises up memories or an old relationship, it doesn't always reveal layers of junk, although it may. Instead, it may simply open those places of loneliness and grief over what I don't have. If I dwell on those thoughts, I get down and spiral toward depression.

To combat those moments, I tell those spirits to leave me alone, and then I remember Psalm 37:4. "Delight yourself in the Lord, and He will give you the desires of your heart."

Not just my desires, but what my heart desires. For a long time, the desire of my mind focused on someone, but the desire of my heart was for something better than my mind could know. I remind myself that God won't give me less than the best, and while my mind might settle, my heart doesn't.

As a word of encouragement, think about the cartoon character Snagglepuss from the *Yogi Bear* show. He always said, "Exit stage left."

That's what you have to tell situations such as loneliness, grief, hatred, frustration, and a lot of hurts from your past. Letting go hurts. Because you've been in the same spot for a long time, those old hurts feel like a comfortable old friend. But they aren't a healthy, good friend. Before you can receive your future, God must heal you from the past.

Tell your past it's over. Exit stage left.

Many of us make a New Year's resolution, and that's not a bad thing. How about having a new day's resolution?

Decide what you need to change about yourself daily. At times, it could be difficult, but a positive change usually is good.

Remember, I can't get upset if a person uses me when I encourage them to do it—even if I don't do it intentionally. Some people won't talk to you when they are up on their feet, but when they fall, here they come. They don't answer my calls unless they need something from me. I had to chop these toxic people out of my life like dead tree branches. I no longer encourage any person to use me. I don't need to please them, and the thrill is gone.

Not everybody will be happy for me, so stop waiting for people to express happiness or being proud of me. Learn how to love and be proud of myself. In all this sorrow of my life, I wanted to understand why God took me through so much of it. He knows who He can trust to remain faithful. Despite it all, quit looking down. Keep looking up and quit focusing on how people feel about me.

Above all, quit focusing on trying to please people and doing everything to make them happy. My heart broke because I wanted people to feel the way I felt. That's still part of my people-pleaser addiction, and I continue letting that go.

Continue learning to please God first and then me. The past is the past and people are who they are. Keep my head up and continue to move forward.

I thought I knew some people. Instead, I know of them. They had spirits connected to them, and those spirits tried to connect to me once I realized who they were. God showed me the spirits on them, and while He tried to expose the truth to me, I kept brushing things off and going back. No more. If God shows me a spirit connected to a person, I exit stage left.

I also learned I can't joke around with everybody. Some people might take my words or actions to a different level. They make take it personally, and I leave them wounded without meaning to. Hurting someone happens when we don't know we did it, so I need to listen to the Holy Spirit and be aware of how others react. If they look offended, I must fix it. If they don't find my jokes funny, they don't have to laugh. Stop judging others for their likes and don't likes, and check yourself. Yep, that's me. I have got to learn how to check myself more for my wrongdoings.

If a person stops talking to me, my emotions run all over the place as I wonder what I did. It could be nothing I did, but it's not always about them either. Sometimes, it is me. Yup, I have to check myself and go to that individual, confess my wrong, and ask them to forgive me. If they don't, at least I did my part.

I learned everybody ain't meant to be in your life forever, because where God is taking me, everybody can't go. You gotta let them go so you can grow. Some people were never meant to be in my life for more than a minute (if at all), but I kept holding on to them until something major happened. Then I tried to fault them. God kept showing me small signs, but I didn't pay attention. I begin to check myself and move on.

Although trivial, an addiction is an addiction. I found myself addicted to chocolate candy and dark soda. Not such a terrible thing—unless I can't go without them and consume too much. If God says give it up, He has reasons, so obey.

I learned to bathe with body wash and wash my clothes with laundry detergent instead of dishwashing liquid. I never knew about using deodorant rather than baking soda, so I learned and made that change. Regardless of what I was taught, I may need to learn something new for myself and all those that interact with me daily.

I want to shout out to everyone who corrected me for pointing out the things I did wrong. Honestly, I appreciate and thank you all. I'd rather have somebody correct me for wrongdoings than go around and talk about me behind my back. Thank you so much, because it teaches me more about what I need to do and not do.

Sometimes, God used people to expose the truth to me. Other times, we tramp through self-exposure even though it hurts like surgery without anesthesia. But he's letting me know, "This thing has to stop. You gotta check yourself!" He has to correct me, and that's the area where I needed deliverance.

Nothing wrong with checking yourself even though it hurts to be corrected—by others and by God. But I'd rather be corrected than continue living with the same junk in me. I thank God for removing that baggage Where He's taking me, that trash can't go.

In wrapping up, this chapter exit reminds me of a blues singer, Tyrone Davis—one of Dad's friends. He sang "I Reached the Turning Point."

Of all I learned during my process of various withdrawals, the most important lesson sounds simple.

You gotta let go of your past and move forward.

No, it's not easy. Yes, yes, yes, it's very painful going through withdrawals, but you gotta go through withdrawals to find healing and grow.

Amid deliverance, withdrawals, and oh so painful healing, remember blessings are coming.

Lord, heal us from any addiction that leaves us unlike Jesus.

Medication Journal

IN TODAY'S WORLD, DOCTORS throw a pill at everything, resulting in a world addicted to drugs. Even prescriptions gain a hold over your body. I'm not saying never take medicine, but your body can become addicted to even the best-intended pill.

Don't think you gotta take prescribed and over-the-counter medication to overcome sickness and disease—especially those with deep, spiritual roots.

Ask yourself, how can I overcome the things God wants to break off me? While it may cause withdrawal, trust that He never abandons us.

> But Zion said, "The LORD has abandoned me, And the Lord has forgotten me."
> Can a woman forget her nursing child and have no compassion on the son of her womb?
> Even these may forget, but I will not forget

you. **"Behold, I have inscribed you on the palms of My hands;** *Your walls are continually before Me."*

Isaiah 49:14-16

On the following pages, I have listed potential addictions. Use the blank space to record your answers. If you need more space, consider using a journal or spiral notebook.

How can I overcome...?

Unforgiveness

Old love

Not forgiving myself

Grief

Gossip, Depression

Complaining, Suicidal thoughts

Relapsing

Fear of moving forward

Talking too much

Finally, how can I focus on the positive?

Works Cited

2005. *DIARY OF A Mad Black Woman*. Directed by Darren Grant. Performed by Tyler Perry Cicely Tyson.

About the Author

TFOUNDER/CEO OF HURT, BROKEN, Now Healed and Delivered Ministries, Teresa Tarpley released her first book in 2016, *HeartBroken: Now Healed and Delivered*. In ministering to other people, Teresa focuses on those coming out of addiction and striving to live a new life with Jesus as their guide.

In 2017, Teresa became a radio talk show host of *Straight Up Radio Talk Show*. Based on her life story, she launched the stage play *I am Beautiful* as the executive producer. Teresa also played a part in the stage play, which opened doors for several minor roles in movies. She became a certified actress.

Recognized for the best stage play executive producer during 2019 in Phoenix, Arizona, Teresa enjoys acting, hoping each role she plays ministers to someone. In addition, she shares her testimony whenever the opportunity arises.

Following the release of her second book in 2021, Teresa continued writing and releasing other books while working as a Certified Nurse Aid, auditioning for parts in various movies, and searching for her family ancestry.

All her books are available at discounted prices for bulk purchases, sales promotions, fund-raising events, or for educational purchases.

For more information about the author, to obtain special pricing or to schedule Teresa as a speaker for your event, please contact Teresa Tarpley by phone or email.

PO Box 50162

Fort Worth, TX 76105

(817) 210-7517

Email: minister.ttarpley@yahoo.com

Other Books By Teresa Tarpley

HeartBroken: Now Healed and Delivered
ISBN: 978-0692583739
Radical Women, 2016

Why Y'all Treat Me So Bad?
ISNB: 978-1734039832
Radical Women, 2021

Mother of Inmates
ISBN: 978-1734039863

Radical Women, 2021

Ain't No Future in the Back
ISBN: 978-1734039887
Radical Women, 2022

Everything's Out in the Open
ISBN: 979-8988648505
Radical Women, 2023

About Radical Women

OWNER OF RADICAL WOMEN, Lisa Bell, lives in Granbury, Texas. She retired early in 2023 from her position as an editor for NOW Magazines, LLC, covering two of nine markets. She still offers freelance editing of all types (including developmental editing), interior design, custom cover creation, and she strives to guide and assist writers in publishing their stories independently or with traditional publishers. Whether fiction or non-fiction, Lisa has experience and knowledge to make a good story great.

Lisa also serves as a coach for two writing groups under the name of Radical Writers. She strives to teach writers the skills of writing so their work becomes the best they can achieve. Through writing groups, individual coaching, editing and more, she takes pride in finished products that rival any book regardless of the publisher.

Lisa has published hundreds of articles and multiple books. To learn more about Lisa, contact her by phone, text, email, or visiting the bylisabell website.

www.bylisabell.com.
(817) 269-9066
lisabell@bylisabell.com
www.texasradicalwriters.com